PICKLEBALL'S BEST EXCUSES

Hilarious Quips Every Pickler Should Know

Joshua Shifrin

Skyhorse Publishing

Copyright © 2025 by Joshua Shifrin

All rights reserved. No part of this book may be reproduced in any manner without the express written consent of the publisher, except in the case of brief excerpts in critical reviews or articles. All inquiries should be addressed to Skyhorse Publishing, 307 West 36th Street, 11th Floor, New York, NY 10018.

Skyhorse Publishing books may be purchased in bulk at special discounts for sales promotion, corporate gifts, fund-raising, or educational purposes. Special editions can also be created to specifications. For details, contact the Special Sales Department, Skyhorse Publishing, 307 West 36th Street, 11th Floor, New York, NY 10018 or info@skyhorsepublishing.com.

Skyhorse® and Skyhorse Publishing® are registered trademarks of Skyhorse Publishing, Inc.®, a Delaware corporation.

Visit our website at www.skyhorsepublishing.com.

Please follow our publisher Tony Lyons on Instagram @tonylyonsisuncertain

10 9 8 7 6 5 4 3 2 1

Library of Congress Cataloging-in-Publication Data is available on file.

Cover design by Kai Texel
Cover and interior artwork by Ian Baker

Print ISBN: 978-1-5107-8214-3
Ebook ISBN: 978-1-5107-8371-3

Printed in China

Contents

Introduction 5

Excuses 9

Epilogue 121

Acknowledgments 123

About the Author 125

Introduction

I love Pickleball! I mean, I really LOVE it! From dinks to dillballs to Falafels and Flapjacks. From matches under a sun-soaked sky to swatting that little plastic ball under the lights at night. I mean honestly, is there a better feeling than a well-played game followed by downing a few cold drinks with your fellow competitors and discussing the intricacies of the contest? Clearly, I'm not the only one who feels this way, and the reasons, at least to me, are obvious. The game is fun, a great workout, a terrific way to meet people, and people can play at any age. And oh my, is it ever addicting! If I had a nickel for every moment I dreamed about my next Pickleball game while at work, well, let's just say that I'd have enough money to stop thinking about playing and to literally go at it to my heart's content.

If you're reading this book, surely you don't need any more convincing. We can all agree that Pickleball is the best thing to

Pickleball's Best Excuses

come along since sliced bread. As the adage goes, "A bad day on the Pickleball court is better than a good day at the office." But is it just me or is this great game just a little bit sweeter, if that's possible, when you come out on top? To the victor comes the spoils and it just feels great to be the king of the court.

But what happens when things don't go exactly your way? When you're so excited that you inadvertently step into the kitchen on too many occasions. Or that day when you are plagued by faults. And then you lose the most crucial point of the day . . . the final point!

When the unthinkable occurs, and you end up on the losing end of the stick, clearly there might be a plausible explanation. And it goes without saying that your athleticism, stamina, or, most importantly, your ability as a Pickler can't be the reason, well, let's just say, you're terrible.

It's been said more than once that in order to maximize one's chances of success, and to make it to the Pickledome, you need to minimize your mistakes. Unfortunately, however, on some days the mishaps just pile up. But as any Pickleballer worth their salt will tell you, there must be a viable (or not so viable) reason for the loss. Perhaps the sun was in your eyes. Or was there a crack on the ball that caused it to bounce off kilter. Of course! It was all your partner's fault. Or was there one of the multitude of reasons you lost that are outlined in this book?

Introduction

The good news is, even on your worst of days when, god forbid, you get "pickled" and don't win a single point, we've got you covered. You now have the resource you need to explain away your worst of defeats. No, you're not a loser. Clearly, you're fit, athletic, good-looking, coordinated, and everybody likes you. So, the next time you go down as dramatically as the *Titanic,* explain away your woeful play with *Pickleball's Best Excuses*!

Excuses

"IF YOU CAN'T STAND THE HEAT, STAY OUT OF THE KITCHEN."

Even a novice Pickleball player will tell you, if you're volleying the ball, you can't step into the kitchen. Yet in the middle of an exciting rally, it can be hard to hold back. We've all been there.

After that little plastic ball goes back and forth, I finally see that sphere loft high and gently up into the air. I go for the smash only to land right into the middle of the kitchen. As a fault is called, I quickly realize my blunder and turn to see my partner giving me the "dagger look."

Alas, if this has happened to you, feel free to explain the gaffe with, "The heat of the moment got to me. Normally I would never hit a ball in the air while in the kitchen."

"THE PING OF THE BALL WAS EXACERBATING MY TINNITUS."

We all know how much fun Pickleball can be. The thrill of a day out with friends and a closely contested match can be the best forty-five minutes of your week. Yet, unbelievably, the game has its naysayers! Yes, there are modern day Scrooges who would like this great game banished altogether. You may be asking yourself, "Why would anyone have a problem with a sport that brings joy to so many?" The constant ping of the ball against the paddle apparently can cause some bystanders to go a bit bonkers.

The good news is you can use this to your advantage. The next time you end up on the losing end, you can always shake hands with your opponents, tell them they played well, and subtly let them know that, "If the ping of the ball hadn't made my tinnitus flare up, we surely would have ended up with the victory."

"My Opponent's Shirt Was the Same Color as the Ball."

There is one often underestimated part of the fun associated with Pickleball: dressing the part. Sure, some of us just go out in sweats or shorts and a T-shirt. But others truly go all out—wristbands, visors, matching outfits, getting all dolled up for the competition can put you in the right frame of mind. However, like anything else in life, there are a few people that take things just a bit too far. Can you say, "neon"!?

The good news is you can use this to your advantage. The next time you're playing an opponent with an outfit that's brighter than the sun and you go down in flames, feel free to tell anyone that will listen, "My opponent's clothes were the same color as the ball, and it was impossible to get a good look."

Pickleball's Best Excuses

"IT'S NOT MY FAULT."

Sure, you can win at Pickleball by being uber aggressive. Going for the lines, hitting with power, and going all out can be effective. But often, it's the player or team with the fewest mistakes that ends up victorious.

As you likely know, an error in Pickleball is called a "fault," which can occur on a serve, hitting the ball into the net, volleying before a ball has bounced on each side, etc. Thus, avoiding "faults" is paramount to a winning recipe.

So, if you minimized your errors yet suffered an embarrassing loss, and you want to use a tried-and-true excuse, just look 'em in the eye and state, "That loss wasn't my fault!"

"My Spouse Made Me Go Shopping This Morning and I Didn't Have Time to Properly Warm Up."

Pickleball takes a lot of skill and practice. To get to the top tier, a player needs athleticism, conditioning, mental stamina, hand-eye coordination, and, of course, hours and hours on the court. Yet, even with the best efforts and genetics, at times, the difference between winning and losing can be razor thin. Therefore, any advantage one can get can be consequential.

I don't know about you, but before a big match, I like to have a good warm up. A good breakfast, proper stretching, and just the right amount of serves, groundstrokes, and volleys are an essential part of my pregame routine.

But what happens when your ritual is disrupted? You're running late and get to the court just in time to hear, "0-0-2," and the next thing you know you're shaking hands on the losing side of the net. Well, fear not, because I've got just the excuse for you. Just feel free to say, "My significant other made me go shopping this morning and it took forever. I barely made it to the match on time and couldn't properly prepare for battle."

"My Partner is Pedantic. He Kept Calling a Penalty on Me Every Time the Toe of My Shoe Touched the Kitchen Line."

With the Pickleball gods as my witnesses, it's not my fault we lost! My partner, bless his heart, is a stickler for the rules. Every time the toe of my shoe so much as grazed the kitchen line, he'd scream "penalty!" like he was auditioning for a role in a courtroom drama. I mean, come on, it's Pickleball, not *Law and Order*!

I'd try to explain that a little toe tap never hurt anyone, but he'd just shake his smug head and cite chapter and verse from the official rulebook. So, there I was, tiptoeing around the court like a ballet dancer, terrified of incurring the wrath of my partner's inner referee.

So, next time you see me hobbling around the court with one foot suspended in mid-air, you can bet I'll say, "It's not clumsiness, it's my strategic avoidance of the dreaded kitchen line. The last thing I need is more grief from my pedantic partner."

Excuses

Did You Know?

There are two theories about how Pickleball got its name. The first theory is that the sport was named after Pickles, the dog of one of the game's co-founders, who loved to chase after the ball. The second is that it was named after the term "pickle boat," referring to the last boat to return with its catch.

"I Was Distracted By the Noise When My Opponents' Paddles Hit the Ball."

My ears! Have you ever listened closely to the cacophony of sounds that erupts when those paddles make contact with the ball? It's like a symphony of screeching cats orchestrated by mischievous squirrels armed with frying pans.

Each ping, pong, and plop sends my brain into a frenzy, trying to decipher if it's a Pickleball game or a drum circle. I found myself frazzled by the rhythmic trance while my opponents effortlessly scored point after point.

And if you've experienced something similar, be sure to say, "With the eardrum-piercing exploding sound, how could anyone be expected to concentrate?"

Excuses

"THE NET IS DEFINITELY HIGHER ON MY SIDE."

I know it seems impossible, but hear me out: The laws of physics seem to warp around me when I step onto the Pickleball court. You see, the net on my side is like a magnet for my shots, pulling them downwards with irresistible force. It's as if the ball has a mind of its own, aiming straight for the net's pinnacle, despite my best efforts to convince it otherwise.

I even tried offering the net a bribe—extra pickle juice, its favorite snack—but alas, it remained steadfast in its high-reaching ways. So please forgive my errant shots. Blame it on the mischievous net conspiring against me. After all, in the grand scheme of Pickleball excuses, this one surely takes the cake . . . or should I say, the pickle?

The good news is that this is such a far-fetched excuse that it seems impossible to make up. Just tell your friends with a good sense of humor, "I don't mean to sound paranoid, but the net clearly has it out for me."

Excuses

"It Was Too Windy."

Trust me, it wasn't my lack of skill that made me miss that shot! It was that terrible low-pressure system from the south. Picture this: I'm about to execute the perfect shot, when suddenly, a gust of wind sweeps in like a tornado on a mission to sabotage my game. The ball veers off course faster than you can say "pickle juice," leaving me standing there with an expression of disappointment that could rival the look on a sad puppy's face.

I tried to explain my swing and miss, but they were too busy laughing at my futile attempt to chalk it up to the elements. I mean, who could blame them? It's not every day you witness a Pickleball player attributing their lackluster performance to Mother Nature's whims.

So, next time you flub a shot, just look your opponents in the eye and say, "Wow, did you feel that sudden gust of wind?!"

"My Opponent Was Serving Really Fast. She Must Have Been Doing Something Illegal."

In the thrilling world we call Pickleball, excuses often serve as the saving grace for those on the losing end. In my recent match, speed became the contentious issue. As the ball whizzed past me at what seemed like a NASCAR speed, I couldn't help but wonder if it was my opponent's skill or some illicit serving technique that tipped the scales. After all, in the world of Pickleball, anything can happen, especially when excuses are on the line.

With each lightning-fast serve, doubts crept in, whispering accusations of foul play. Surely, no one could possess such blistering speed without bending the rules. My opponent's serves felt more like missiles launched from a secret arsenal than fair shots within the bounds of the game.

Despite my best efforts, I found myself struggling to keep up, constantly on the defensive. But fear not, if you find yourself in a similar predicament, feel free to tell anyone who will listen, "If my opponent wasn't constantly violating the serving rules, I would have wiped the floor with them."

"I Can't Keep Dinking Shot After Shot. It's So Boring!"

Listen here, my dear Pickleball comrades, it's not that I lack the passion for this terrific game. Not even remotely, but sometimes it's just so monotonous. That incessant *dink* really gets to me sometimes, as if each gentle tap is tearing out a little piece of my soul.

While everyone else is lost in the fervor of the rally, I'm waging a silent battle against the relentless repetition. It's like *Groundhog Day* but with visors and paddles!

I yearn for the days when I could unleash a mighty swing, and the ball would soar across the court like a cheetah chasing its prey. Alas, for now, I'm resigned to the fate of a dinking disciple, forever seeking solace in the occasional rogue lob or unexpected smash.

So please forgive my reluctance to engage in this dinkathon—an existential quest for excitement in an ocean of dinks! So, the next time you die a slow death administered by those softly hit shots, just say, "I miss the day of power Pickleball. I'd rather lose than dink all day like a ninety-eight-pound weakling."

"Why Do You Have to Serve Underhand? It Gives Your Opponent the Advantage. Tennis Rules Make Much More Sense."

Why, oh why, must we serve underhand in this great game of Pickleball? It's like asking a bear to roar softly! Underhand serves feel like we're politely offering our opponents a free ticket to smashville.

I mean, seriously, where's the drama? Where's the power? It's like serving up a balloon and saying, "Here you go, please return with vigor!"

In tennis, you can unleash your inner Wimbledon warrior with a thunderous overhead serve that strikes fear into the hearts of your opponents. But in Pickleball? We're stuck with this dainty underhand nonsense.

So next time my opponent smacks a winner off my feeble underhand serve, I won't blame my lack of skill. No! I'll blame the rules for robbing me of my serving swagger and I'll say loud and proud, "The rules in tennis certainly make much more sense!"

"It Was Too Cold Today."

Chilly weather makes me more like a frozen pickle than a nimble player on the Pickleball court. Every time I swing my paddle, it felt like my joints are freezing in place. And I mean, who can focus on hitting that perfect shot when your fingers are icicles, and your nose is running like a broken pipe?

I swear, I tried everything! I wore plenty of layers. I danced around like a cast member of *Footloose*. I even tried some impromptu jumping jacks between points. However, in the end, my efforts were futile against the icy grip of Old Man Winter.

So, if your shots lacked their usual pinpoint accuracy, and your footwork resembled that of a clumsy polar bear, just remember to blame it on the cold! After all, even the professional Pickleballers can't play well when they feel like a snowman. So, the next time your game goes as south as the South Pole, just explain it with, "It was freezing out there!"

Did You Know?

The ball used in Pickleball is similar to a wiffle ball, with holes through it. Forty-hole Pickleballs are used for outdoor and twenty-six-hole Pickleballs are used for indoor use.

"My Partner Hits Overheads Too Softly. It's Like He's Afraid of Hurting the Ball."

You know, it's a curious thing really, and I'm having a hard time figuring it out. My partner, bless their heart, approaches overhead shots with the gentle grace of a butterfly landing on a flower in a meadow. It's almost poetic, really. But alas, in the heat of the game, we found ourselves at a slight disadvantage. You see, while their intention is noble—presumably preserving the integrity of the ball's feelings—it does tend to lack the necessary *oomph* to bring about a victory.

We lost, not because of skill disparity, no! It was more of a clash between sportsmanship and the desire for victory. So, as much as I appreciate their concern for the ball's well-being, perhaps a gentle reminder that it's okay to give it a little tough love next time might be in order.

Until then, we'll just chalk it up to an overabundance of kindness in a fiercely competitive world. The good news, however, is you can use your partner's gentle touch to explain your team's defeat by saying, "If my partner wasn't so worried about breaking the ball in half, maybe we could have won a few more points."

"My Partner Always Gives Our Opponents the Benefit of the Doubt on Line Calls. I Keep Telling Him There's No Place for Integrity in this Game!"

Ah, the eternal struggle between sportsmanship and ruthless competition rears its head yet again! My partner, who must have a virtuous soul, insists on granting our opponents the benefit of the doubt on every line call as if they were Mother Teresa with a Pickleball paddle.

But alas, I find myself repeatedly reminding them that in this cutthroat world of court battles, there's simply no room for such noble gestures! After all, a win is a win, regardless of how it's achieved. Yet, try as I might, my partner remains steadfast in their commitment to fairness.

I just don't get it.

If you've experienced a similar scenario, the next time victory slips through your fingers, don't blame your lack of skill, but rather your partner's unwavering dedication to sportsmanship. And of course, tell anyone that will listen, "If it wasn't for my partner's insatiable desire for fairness, the outcome surely would have been better."

"My Back Hurt from Carrying My Partner."

One of the best decisions one can make in this great sport is whom to pick as a partner. Sure, you can have skill, athleticism, tenacity, but if your partner is a clumsy novice, you'll likely be out of luck.

Let's use our sister sport of tennis as a guide. Make sure that your teammate is top notch. If you're Serena, you better find your Venus if you want to bring home the gold.

The good news, however, is that if your partner happens to be subpar, you can use this to your advantage. The next time all the mistakes come from your teammate's side of the court, how about uttering, "We could have won but my back was beginning to hurt from carrying my weaker half."

"Who Was the Moron Who Came Up with the Idea of the Kitchen? How Are You Supposed to Get to the Net to Hit Winners?"

Who was the genius—or should I say, *the absolute idiot*—who came up with the idea of the kitchen? Seriously, how are you supposed to "rush and crush" at the net when you've got this arbitrary "no-go zone" looming over you like a dark cloud?

It's like trying to eat soup with a fork! Every time I try to make my triumphant charge to the net, I'm rudely reminded that I'm not allowed to step foot in the kitchen. Well, excuse me for wanting to be where the action is!

Honestly, if I had a nickel for every time that cursed kitchen thwarted my plans for Pickleball domination, I'd be rich enough to retire and play Pickleball day and night. But until then, I'll just have to keep making excuses.

"Why in the world did the inventors of this great game implement that pesky little rectangle?"

Did You Know?

Pickleball was invented in 1965 on Bainbridge Island, Washington.

"My Opponent Kept Lobbing the Ball Over My Head When I Rushed the Net. That Isn't Fair!"

Ever feel like your opponent has a secret pact with Pickleball gods? That's how I felt on the Pickleball court today. Every time I dare to rush the net with dreams of victory, my opponent's deft lobs soar overhead like they were interviewing for a spot in the aviation industry. It was like playing against a professional skydiver rather than a fellow Pickleball enthusiast.

I mean, come on! Where's the fairness in that? I barely have time to get near the kitchen before I have to scramble back to the baseline to retrieve another wayward lob.

So, if my performance seemed more like a game of "Whack-a-Mole" than a strategic sport, blame it on the unfair alliance between my opponent and the stratosphere. Next time, I'm bringing a ladder—or maybe a trampoline! But at least I can tell anyone that will listen, "The only reason I lost is due to all of those lofty lobs."

Pickleball's Best Excuses

"My Partner Distracted Me with Too Much Chit-Chat."

Today's Pickleball match turned into a battle of wits against my partner's unstoppable verbal barrage. It was like playing doubles with a talk show host who talks over all their guests. Every shot I attempted was accompanied by a running commentary about their weekend plans, the latest gossip, and their Aunt Mildred's pet parrot. I barely had time to focus on the game amidst the never-ending chatter. I mean, who knew Aunt Mildred's parrot had such a colorful vocabulary?

So, if my serves went wide or my volleys went haywire, blame it on the non-stop chatterbox beside me. Lesson learned: Next time, I'm bringing earplugs or signing my partner up for a stand-up comedy gig so they can get it all out before the match—anything to help me focus on the game! But if this happens to you, and it likely has, you can explain your woeful play with, "How could I possibly focus with all of that incessant chit-chat?"

"I Got Nervous Because Too Many People Were Watching My Match."

Let me tell you, this wasn't just any ordinary game of Pickleball. The stakes were high, the tension palpable, and the audience? Well, let's just say they were as plentiful as pickles in a jar!

As I initially stepped onto the court, I felt strong, confidence oozing from every pore. But then it hit me like a ton of bricks. I couldn't help but notice the sea of eager faces, all eyes fixated on my every move. Suddenly, my knees turned to jelly, my grip faltered, and my serves resembled that of a four-year-old.

Blame it on the pressure, blame it on the spotlight, but most importantly, blame it on the fact that I was convinced the crowd was secretly comprised of Pickleball aficionados, scrutinizing my every move with the intensity of the most seasoned critics.

So yes, I may have lost the match, but hey, at least I have a built-in excuse.

"If all of those discerning eyes weren't judging my every move, I surely would have played much better."

"My Visor Kept Slipping Down So I Couldn't See the Ball."

Ah, the plight of the perpetually stylish Pickleball player! You see, my visor wasn't just any ordinary headgear; it was a top-of-the-line fashion statement, designed to dazzle my opponent with its sheer elegance. However, in its quest for sartorial perfection, it occasionally decided to moonlight as a blindfold, plunging me into a world of uncertainty where the ball became as elusive as a shot in the dark.

As I stumbled around the court, desperately fumbling with my visor, my opponent must have thought they were facing off against a lost pirate searching for buried treasure! But fear not, because if this happens to you, clearly you have an excuse at the ready.

"If it wasn't for my fashion faux pas, I clearly would have won."

Did You Know?

Pickleball is the fastest-growing sport in the United States.

Excuses

My Hat Was Too Big. It Kept Flying Off."

Per the last excuse, you now know what to do if your visor is causing you problems. But if you're old school and would never wear a wimpy visor, and a tough guy hat is your preferred headgear of choice: Never fear! We have the perfect excuse for you as well.

Let's just say that you're sporting the perfect cap, but as you sprint to that little plastic sphere your hat continually refuses to stay on your head. Point after point, you find yourself with one hand on your paddle and the other holding your headgear.

If this sounds like you, and the ending result is a big "L," just look your opponent in the eye and say, "If it wasn't for the fact that my hat was two sizes too big, I'm sure I could have given you a better contest."

"What's With the Stupid Scoring System? '1-0-1,' '2-2-2,' '5-2-1.' It's Way Too Confusing."

I mean, seriously, who came up with this mathematical madness? Was it a scientist with a wicked sense of humor? Or just someone with a vendetta against simplicity?

I'm on the court, sweating bullets, trying to keep track of who's winning and what the score is. Suddenly, my brain starts doing mental gymnastics trying to decode these cryptic numbers while simultaneously trying to hit a tiny ball over a net. It's like trying to solve a Rubik's cube while riding a unicycle!

And don't even get me started on the arguments it causes. "No, no, no, it's 5-2-1, not 2-5-1!" It's like we need a referee just to keep track of the score.

So yeah, you have an easy excuse. "This scoring method is insane. Who can focus with this crazy system?"

"I Got Caught in Traffic and Was Late for My Match So I Had No Time to Warm Up."

You see, it wasn't just any traffic. It was a conga line of turtles on scooters, elderly folks practicing synchronized lane changes, and a rogue ice cream truck that was lost in a maze of one-way streets. I tried everything to speed things up—waving my paddle like a magic wand, honking my horn to the rhythm of "Eye of the Tiger," even attempting to negotiate with a particularly stubborn pigeon—but alas, this was no ordinary traffic. This was Traffic Plus!

By the time I arrived at the court, I was as tight as a drum and about as flexible as a garden gnome. My opponent was already volleying like a pro, while I stumbled onto the court like a newborn giraffe on roller skates. So, you see, it wasn't my fault I lost; but at least I could explain it.

"My horrendous play was due to those dawdling tortoises and that darn ice cream truck."

"I Forgot to Wear My Lucky Shirt."

You know, it's like this: every time I don my trusty shirt, I transform into a Pickleball powerhouse, slicing through the competition with the finesse of a cucumber ninja. But, on that fateful day, in a moment of sheer forgetfulness, I left it hanging in the closet, much to my chagrin.

As I stepped onto the court, I felt naked, scared, vulnerable. My opponents sensed my shirtless sorrow and exploited it mercilessly, sending balls whizzing past me with the precision of homing missiles. It wasn't just a game of Pickleball; it was a battle against fate itself.

In hindsight, I realize my mistake. It wasn't just a shirt; it was a shield against defeat. So, the next time your game plummets faster than a mob informant with cement shoes, explain it with, "I simply can't play without my lucky shirt."

"I Had a Hangnail on My Pinky So I Couldn't Hold the Paddle Right."

Listen, I'm all for maintaining a solid grip on life, but when a hangnail decides to crash the Pickleball party, what's a player to do? There I was, ready to unleash my killer serves and dazzling groundstrokes, when suddenly, it felt like a tiny demon was tap-dancing on my cuticle.

Every time I tried to grip the paddle, the tiniest agony pulsed through my finger. My shots veered off course like deflating balloons, and my opponents must have thought they stumbled upon a newbie with two left feet.

I attempted to tape it, band-aid it, charm it, even reason with it, but that hangnail had other plans. So, in the end, I blame not my skills, but the rebellious hangnail that hijacked my game and turned it into a comedy of errors. But at least I explained it with, "If it wasn't for that pesky hangnail, I obviously would have dominated."

"My Shoes Were Too Big."

In the topsy-turvy world of Pickleball excuses, this is a tale of woe that starts at the ground level—literally. Try to picture the following: a crucial match, tension thick enough to slice like a pickle spear, and there I am, ready to unleash my legendary skills. But fate, it seems, had a different plan.

Mid-rally, disaster struck, and you guessed it . . . my shoes failed me! Yes, my new shoes ended up being a size too large. And I was in trouble faster than you can say, "I tripped over my two left feet." Blame it on the wide shoes, blame it on my narrow feet, but the truth remains: my new online footwear order mutinied, leaving me to awkwardly shuffle across the court.

So, forgive my lackluster performance. I was but a victim of fashion's fickle ways. Fear not, for I now have another great excuse: "With new shoes, I shall rise from the ashes like a Pickleball phoenix, ready to conquer the court once more!"

"My Shoes Were Too Tight."

As I stepped onto the Pickleball court, I felt a twinge of panic. My shoes, once snug, had suddenly transformed into foot-binding torture devices! With each shot, my toes cried out in protest, pleading for liberation from their leather prison.

Did my opponents understand my plight? Oh no, they just saw a clumsy dancer, tripping over imaginary obstacles, as if performing a comedic routine for their entertainment.

"It's not my lack of coordination, it's the shoes!" I tried to explain. "They're squeezing the life out of my lower extremities!" But alas, my words were drowned out by the laughter echoing across the court.

So, there I was, hobbling around like a penguin, all because of my shoes. But hey, at least it gave me a good excuse. "Maybe next time, I'll remember to bring shoes that actually fit. And don't even get me started on my socks!"

"I Forgot My Sunscreen, So I Kept Worrying about Getting Fried."

The perils of Pickleball under the scorching sun! Try to picture this: A match of epic proportions, with sweat dripping like a leaky faucet and tension thick enough to pickle cucumbers. Yet, as I stepped onto the court, a horrifying realization sunk in—I had forgotten my sunscreen! While my opponents focused on their serves, groundstrokes, and volleys, I was preoccupied with visions of turning into a human lobster.

With every passing point, my mind was consumed with thoughts of my skin turning into crispy bacon rather than smacking the ball to victory. Blame it on my forgetful nature, but the truth remains: I was more concerned with SPF than being MVP. So, forgive my lack of focus, for I was but a sunburnt soul adrift in a sea of Pickleball paddles. Next time, I'll remember the SPF and leave the worrying to the cucumbers! At least I can tell my dermatologist, "If I had remembered my sunscreen, I surely would have brought home the trophy."

"THE FENCE WAS TOO CLOSE TO THE COURT. I WAS AFRAID OF RUNNING INTO IT."

As we all know, Pickleball is a booming sport. And with the increased demand from players and fans all over the world, the industry is trying to keep pace. And that includes building more courts.

But, as Uncle Sam will tell you, money doesn't grow on trees and it seems that everywhere you turn, space is limited. You may be asking yourself, "What's the answer?" Pack in as many courts as possible into what, at times, seems like a shoebox, with the surrounding barriers seemingly inches away from the baseline and sideline.

The good news is one can use this dimensional dilemma to their advantage. The next time I stop short to avoid running into the fence, only to watch my opponent's winner zip by, you better believe I'm going to say, "If the fence wasn't so close, you'd better believe the outcome would have been different."

Excuses

"THE PLAYERS NEXT TO ME KEPT HITTING THEIR BALL ONTO OUR COURT."

So, I'm poised for Pickleball greatness, ready to dazzle the court with my moves, when suddenly, it starts raining balls from the neighboring court like a bizarre meteor shower. The players next to me seemed to have mistaken our court for a target practice range, their wayward shots landing with alarming accuracy right in the middle of our game, seemingly every time I'm about to hit a winner.

With each stray ball, my concentration shattered like a dropped pickle jar. I tried to dodge, I tried to rally, but it was more like playing dodgeball with a twist than a Pickleball match. In a moment of desperation, I had to pull out the ultimate excuse: "I couldn't perform up to my usual greatness because the players next to me kept hitting their ball onto our court!"

Did You Know?

National Pickleball Day is celebrated on August 8 of each year.

"The Players Next to Me Were Too Noisy."

As I stepped onto the Pickleball court, armed with determination and a paddle, I was ready for victory. But fate had other plans. The moment I stepped onto the court, I realized I was in for a pickle of a situation. The players next to me seemed to have mistaken the venue for a rock concert, their cheers and banter echoing louder than a herd of elephants tap dancing in stilettos.

With each swing, their cacophony reached new heights, throwing me off my game entirely. I tried to concentrate, but it was like trying to meditate in the middle of a fireworks display. In desperation, I had to resort to covering my ears with my hands, making it exceedingly difficult to swing the paddle. The good news . . . I had a great excuse for losing.

"I couldn't focus because the players next to me were too darn noisy!"

"A Bird Landed on My Head. I Needed a Haircut and I Guess He Thought It Was a Nest."

Just as I was about to unleash my killer instinct, nature intervened. A bird swooped down and, mistaking my unkempt mop for prime real estate, decided to make a pit stop right on my noggin. Talk about a feather-brained excuse!

As the other players stared in disbelief, I found myself caught between laughter and mild panic, trying to shoo away my unexpected avian visitor without disturbing the game. Alas, my attempts at diplomacy failed miserably, and I had to resort to the only excuse I could think of that fit the bill: "Sorry folks, a bird landed on my head. I needed a haircut, and I guess he thought it was a nest!"

"I Was Wearing a Cheap Pair of Sunglasses, and They Caused My Vision to go Haywire!"

Little did I know that my choice of eyewear would lead to a comedy of errors. With each serve, I squinted through the cheap lenses of my bargain-bin shades, mistaking my opponent's shots for UFOs and volleying invisible little plastic spheres. My partner, bewildered by my erratic swings, suspected foul play, or perhaps a sudden infatuation with interpretive dance.

But fear not, fellow players, for in my quest to conquer my inadequate vision, I inadvertently mastered the art of dodging imaginary projectiles with finesse. So, while my sunglasses may have been cheap, my excuse for my performance was worth its weight in laughter—a tale of optical illusions and Pickleball confusion that will go down in court history. And of course, the best news is I now have a built-in excuse: "If I had adequate eyewear we surely would have won."

"I WATCHED A VIDEO OF ANDRE AGASSI PLAYING PICKLEBALL WITH A TWO-HANDED BACKHAND. WHEN I TRIED IT, IT DIDN'T WORK OUT SO WELL FOR ME."

In a moment of inspiration (or sheer madness), I decided to channel my inner Agassi on the Pickleball court. Armed with a paddle and determination, I attempted the legendary Andre two-handed backhand. Alas, instead of replicating Agassi's finesse, I resembled Bambi on ice.

As my opponents exchanged bewildered glances, I persisted, convinced that this unorthodox technique would revolutionize the sport. However, reality struck harder than a misplaced smash, and I found myself hitting balls into the stratosphere or, worse, into the net.

So, forgive my folly. While Agassi may be a tennis legend, his Pickleball prowess remains a slippery dream—one I shall leave to YouTube highlights. But at least I can explain my woeful play by stating, "Agassi's two-handed backhand may work well on the tennis court, but in Pickleball it's for the birds."

"I Didn't Drink Water Before My Match, and I Got Dehydrated."

Rule of thumb: Make sure to hydrate. I once decided to enter a match without a single sip of water. As the game progressed, I soon realized that my dehydration was turning me into a human pickle—shriveled, salty, and decidedly less agile.

With each shot, I felt my energy wane, and my paddle became heavier than a giant jar of pickles. My opponent, sensing my plight, kindly offered me a cucumber sandwich in solidarity.

But alas, no amount of crunchy snacks could revive me from my dehydrated daze. I stumbled across the court, resembling less of a Pickleball player and more of a wilted gherkin in distress.

So, dear comrades, let this be a cautionary tale: Hydrate thyself before taking to the court, lest you end up in a pickle of your own making. Yet, if you do find yourself in a similar pickle, how about uttering, "I'd pay a king's ransom for some Gatorade!"

"I DRANK TOO MUCH WATER BEFORE MY MATCH AND I NEEDED TO PEE WHILE I WAS PLAYING."

Per the previous excuse, you now know what to do if you drank too little before the match. But what happens if the opposite is true? Let's just say, in a misguided attempt to stay hydrated, I chugged water like it was going out of style before stepping onto the Pickleball court. Little did I know, I was setting myself up for a watery disaster of epic proportions.

As the pressure of the match intensified, so did the pressure in my bladder, reminding me of its presence with each vigorous rally. With every lunge and sprint, I prayed for a break in the action, a moment of reprieve to dash to the nearest restroom.

But Pickleball waits for no one, and neither does my bladder. In a desperate bid for relief, I resorted to the age-old tactic of the pee-pee dance, much to the bewilderment of my opponents.

So, dear Pickleball pals, let this be a cautionary tale: Hydration is crucial, but moderation is key, unless you want your game to turn into a high stakes battle of bladder control. Still, a great excuse nonetheless. If you find yourself in a similar predicament, as you're running to the bathroom, yell over your shoulder, "I would shake your hand like a good loser after a match, but I really have to pee."

"My Lucky Socks Were Dirty."

I'm about to leave the house and hit the court, feeling unstoppable, when I realize a catastrophic mistake: I opened my sock drawer and my lucky socks—the secret to all my victories—were nowhere to be found! Panic sets in as I scour my room, only to discover they're buried at the bottom of the laundry basket, drowning in a sea of dirt and filth.

Now, faced with the prospect of playing sockless, I'm like a superhero stripped of their powers! Every serve becomes a gamble, every groundstroke a leap of faith. It's like playing Pickleball on a tightrope without a safety net. So, if you witnessed my less-than-stellar performance on the court that day, just remember, "It wasn't my lack of skill, it was the absence of my lucky socks throwing off the delicate balance of the Pickleball universe!"

Did You Know?

Pickleball is now included in physical education programs in schools across the United States.

"I Kept Slamming the Ball at My Opponents, But it Didn't Help Because They Were Good Volleyers."

Ever had one of those days where every shot you make seems to come back to bite you? Well, picture this: I kept slamming the ball at my opponents, thinking I was channeling my inner Pickleball powerhouse. But lo and behold, it wasn't my lack of skill, oh no! I was smacking that plastic sphere with power and precision.

It turns out they were expert volleyers! It was like playing against a team of ninja picklers, gracefully returning every ball with uncanny precision. But at least I have a good excuse. "I was hitting like a powerful gorilla, but my opponents were volleying like John McEnroe in his prime. There was nothing that anyone could have done."

"My Opponents Were Trash Talking and It Got to Me."

Ever been in a match where the banter was as intense as the gameplay? If so, perhaps you've been in a similar situation: I'm on the Pickleball court, feeling like a champ, until my opponents start slinging insults faster than they return shots.

"Nice serve . . . for a beginner!" they quip.

Suddenly, my focus wavers, my serves wobble, and my returns go AWOL.

Why? Well, it's simple: their trash talk was so distracting, it practically had its own gravitational pull! I mean, how can one possibly concentrate on hitting the ball when there's a barrage of snarky remarks flying around? It's like trying to juggle flaming torches while balancing on a unicycle—utterly impossible!

So, next time you see me falter on the court, just remember, "It's not my lack of skill, it's their verbal assault that directly led to my poor performance!"

"My Opponent Was Making the Worst Calls."

Due to my exceptional skill and ability, I clearly don't need to play it safe. You see, when I'm ripping groundstrokes, crushing serves, or popping volleys, I normally aim for the lines. Unfortunately, I was playing in the club championship against my nemesis who goes by the motto, "When in doubt, call it out."

It seemed that every time one of my pinpoint shots would skid off the lines I would hear the "Out" call. By the time I called for a line judge, the damage was done, and I ended up holding the dreaded runner-up trophy.

But don't you worry, when I was retelling the story of the match over a couple of brewskies with my friends, I was sure to tell all of them, "I definitely would have won, but that guy was just making the worst calls."

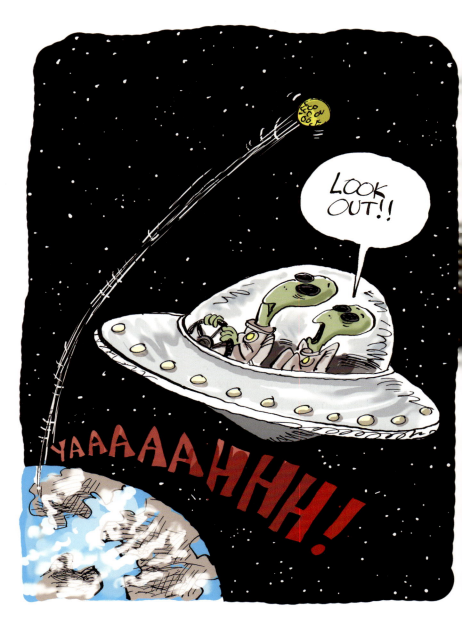

"My Partner's Backhand is Other Worldly."

"Sorry, I can't play today, my partner's backhand is out of this world."

You see, every time she swings, it's like sticking a fork in my eye. Her backhand is so powerful, it's been mistaken for a meteor shower by nearby astronomers. And the sound it makes? Let's just say, the local wildlife has started wearing earplugs.

I'd love to join you on the Pickleball court, but I fear for the safety of innocent bystanders and unsuspecting young children. Last time we played, her backhand sent a ball soaring into the stratosphere, and rumor has it, it's still orbiting Earth. So, the next time we go down in defeat, you can bet I'll be telling anyone who will listen, "If my partner could have hit a decent backhand, we surely would have won."

"I Sprained My Wrist So I Had to Play Left-Handed."

Get this: I'm in the middle of a fierce match, when suddenly, disaster strikes! I sprain my wrist in the most epic of ways—falling face first over my own two feet, of course. Now, faced with the choice of forfeiting or soldiering on, I opt for the latter, because, well, Pickleball waits for no one, and because I'm a tough guy!

But here's the kicker: I'm a righty, and that's the wrist I sprained, leaving me with no choice but to play left-handed. It's like trying to sing at Carnegie Hall with laryngitis: awkward, clumsy, and downright comical! So, if you witnessed my left-handed antics on the court, just remember, "It wasn't a lack of skill, it was my rebellious wrist causing all the chaos!"

"THE PICKLEBALL COURT'S TOO SMALL."

As everyone knows, I'm a terrific tennis player (just ask me). So, I obviously stride onto the Pickleball court with the confidence of a seasoned tennis pro, ready to dominate. But wait—what's this? The court looks suspiciously smaller than I remember! Turns out, I've fallen victim to the dreaded "court shrinkage" phenomenon.

Blame it on muscle memory or a touch of selective vision, but navigating the compact Pickleball court suddenly feels like playing tennis in a shoebox. Every swing is a delicate dance to avoid colliding with the sidelines, and don't even get me started on the kitchen—it's like trying to squeeze into skinny jeans after a holiday feast! So, if you witnessed my awkward maneuvers and errant shots, just remember, "It wasn't my lack of skill, it was the sneaky contraction of the Pickleball court!

"There Was a Leaf on the Court, and I Couldn't Concentrate."

With every genius, there normally comes a bit of madness. In my experience, this statement holds true on the Pickleball court as well. Many Pickleball aficionados seem to be perfectionists. From the perfect outfit to the textbook grip on their paddles, everything needs to be just right.

If this sounds like you, the next time you're playing in the fall, and you come down on the losing end of the ledger, feel free to shake your opponent's hand and say, "Congratulations on the victory, but to be honest I really just couldn't concentrate at all with all of those leaves on the court."

"I Skipped Church This Week and God is Getting Back at Me."

As I started to warm-up, I couldn't help but feel a divine retribution looming over me. You see, this past Sunday, I chose the cozy embrace of my blankets over the solemn pews of the church. And now, it seems the Almighty has decided to use my Pickleball game as a divine punishment.

With every missed shot and every unfortunate bounce, I couldn't shake the feeling that a higher power was behind it all, teaching me a lesson in the most unconventional way possible. "Forgive me, O Mighty Creator, for my backhand lacks conviction!" I cried out, hoping for a celestial intervention.

But alas, my prayers went unanswered, and I was left to face the consequences of my Sunday morning slumber. Lesson learned: next time, I'll trade my Pickleball paddle for a pew! But at least I can tell all my laughing competitors, "I skipped church and clearly God is getting back at me."

"Sweat Got in My Eyes."

Picture the following: A fierce game of Pickleball under the scorching sun. Beads of perspiration run with abandon down my sun-scorched forehead, gravity pulling them toward my eyes with each passing second. When I fail to wipe my brow, it leaks into the corner of my eyes and the salty burn stings, quickly impairing my vision.

As I stumble blindly across the court, my opponents watch in bewildered amusement, wondering if I had mistaken the game for a game of Pin the Tail on the Donkey.

"It's not my fault!" I exclaim, attempting to rub the sweat from my eyes. "The sweat betrayed me!"

Despite my most valiant of efforts, I couldn't see, and victory eluded me. Lesson learned: Next time, I will surely invest in industrial-strength goggles. And if that fails me too, I'll just quip, "With all this sweat in my eyes, I couldn't see!"

"I Lost a Contact Lens."

In Pickleball, that are a lot of essential elements needed to be successful. You need practice, athleticism, stamina, and, as evidenced by the last excuse, you clearly need visual acuity. If you're like many of the readers of this book, you very well may need a little man-made help to track that little plastic ball. Whether it's glasses or contacts, as we get older, a little visual assistance is often a necessity.

If you've been reading this book, I'm sure you've figured out by now that many times our Achilles heel can be exactly what we need to get us out of Dodge. So, the next time you're shaking hands at the net with a pitiful look on your face, hold your free hand to your eye and say, "I lost a contact lens midway through the first game, but you know me . . . I never quit."

"My Glasses Were Dirty."

As I stepped onto the Pickleball court, I quickly realized that my vision was about as clear as a jar of sand at the beach. Blaming my dirty glasses seemed like the perfect excuse for my clumsy footwork and mistimed swings.

With each point lost, I cursed the smudges on my lenses, which seemed to multiply faster than the balls flying past me. I attempted to wipe them clean on my shirt, but only succeeded in smearing them more.

If only there were mini windshield wipers! In the end, my attempts to see the ball clearly were futile, and my opponents capitalized on my blurry vision with merciless precision.

"If it weren't for my dirty glasses, I would have definitely been victorious."

Did You Know?

Pickleball players come from a diverse age range. About 75 percent of avid players (those who play eight or more times a year) are under the age of fifty-five, dispelling the myth that it's only a game for seniors.

"I Was Worried My Opponent Was Going to Hit Me with His Serve."

As the match got underway, one of my opponent's powerful forehands hit me right in the gut. Then, a few points later, his supersonic serve nearly took my head off. I found myself backing up further and further to protect my livelihood until my back was nearly up against the fence.

By the end of the match, as I was going down in flames, I was just trying to get off the court without losing a limb. Although the loss stung, the pain would have been a lot worse if I continuously got pegged with the ball. And at least I could explain my demise with, "I know I lost, but I 'm just happy I didn't lose my life."

"I'm Not Used to This Paddle."

If you're like many of us, you believe all that practice and hard work is for the birds, especially when you can try to buy yourself a better game. And in Pickleball that starts with a new and improved paddle. I show up to the court with a brand-new, state-of-the-art weapon, sleek and shiny as a sports car fresh off the lot. But alas, as soon as the game starts, it's like trying to wield a kettlebell.

Suddenly, every shot feels like I'm swinging with weights on my hands. My serves veer off course like they're puppies chasing after pigeons, and my forehands and backhands . . . let's just say my opponent would likely have no problem handling them with their eyes closed.

So, when you see me walking off the course with my head hung low and my spirit depleted, you'll surely hear me mutter, "I'm just not used to this paddle."

"I Need a New Paddle."

The game is on, adrenaline pumping, when suddenly, my trusty paddle emits a distressing creak. With a dramatic flourish, I stand tall and proclaim to my opponents, "Alas, my faithful paddle has served its last shot! It yearns for retirement in the hallowed halls of Pickleball history."

My opponents may appear skeptical, yet I continue, "But fear not! With a new paddle, I shall rise like a phoenix from the ashes of defeat, ready to conquer the courts once more!" And thus, dear readers, the excuse transforms from a mere plea for mercy to a rallying cry for Pickleball glory. And remember to say, "Once I save up a few dollars, I'm definitely going to buy a new paddle."

"I Couldn't Focus."

Ah, the plight of the easily distracted Pickleball player! I step onto the court, mind sharp as a tack, ready to take home another win, when, out of nowhere, a flash of color catches the corner of my eye. A butterfly flutters by, effortlessly flapping in the wind, and suddenly my attention is gone faster than a dink shot down the line.

Next thing I know, I'm mesmerized by the clouds drifting overhead, contemplating the meaning of life while my opponent effortlessly racks up points. Birds chirp, spectators sneeze, and all I can think about is what's for lunch and why that one cloud looks like a giant "L."

Clearly, I need to take some ADHD medication and bring some noise-canceling headphones and blinders! But at least I can explain my woeful play with, "I don't know what happened today. I simply couldn't focus."

I Went Out Last Night and Now I'm Hungover.

With a groan and a wince, I slumped out of my car with my dark sunglasses, greasy breakfast sandwich, and a colossal jug of water. My partner, looking concerned at my clearly dehydrated form, asked if I was okay.

I explained, "I got a little carried away last night . . . I had one too many picklebacks. Let's just say, my forehand and backhand won't be the only thing feeling pickled."

As my partner's eyebrows shot up, I continued, "I must've thought I was a Pickleball prodigy, taking shots like I was aiming for the Olympics. But alas, this morning, I woke up feeling like I'd been hit by a rogue serve.

"So, if my game is a bit off today, blame it on the brine. I promise, I'll stick to the court next time and leave the pickling for our opponents!"

The good news is if you've ever found yourself in a pickle similar to this, just explain it with, "I knew I shouldn't have had that last one."

"THE WEATHER WAS HORRIBLE."

As I stepped onto the Pickleball court, I was greeted by an overcast, stormy sky that seemed determined to rain on my parade—and my game—quite literally. Blaming the weather seemed like the perfect excuse for my less-than-stellar performance. With each gust of wind, my shots went wildly off course, as if Mother Nature herself was playing against me.

I tried to be precise, but with the wind it was like playing against a tornado in sneakers! If only I could convince my opponents to agree that a monsoon was the ultimate handicap. Alas, my Pickleball prowess was no match for the unpredictable forces of nature. So, next time you see me slipping and sliding on the court, you can just bet I'll say, "It's the weather's fault—for being so darn unpredictable!"

"My Sunglasses Kept Slipping Off of My Nose."

"Okay, I know what it looks like," I say, as I adjust my sunglasses for the umpteenth time. But believe me, it's not my fault my game resembled a scene from *The Matrix*.

As my opponent raised an eyebrow, I launched into my excuse. "You see, my sunglasses decided they were on vacation, slipping off my nose like a kid on a waterslide. Every serve, every groundstroke, every volley, they were doing their own limbo dance, aiming for my chin."

I tried everything—sticky tape, double-sided tape, even a dab of pickle juice for good measure—but those shades just wouldn't cooperate.

So, if you saw me squinting like a far-sighted fool trying to read small print, blame it on the rogue shades. Next time, I'll make sure they're securely fastened, or maybe just invest in a pair with a better grip! And if this has ever happened to you, just let anyone who will listen know, "I surely would have played better if I had a properly fitting pair of sunglasses."

Excuses

"I WAS SO INCONSISTENT."

I'm normally the picture of consistency. Many of my opponents have stated that playing against me is like playing against a brick wall. And why not? As most instructors will tell you, more points are lost by missed easy shots than are won with winners.

But what happens when there is simply an off day? When, despite my best efforts, nothing is going right? My serves are hitting the net, my groundstrokes are flying long, and don't even get me started on my net game!

We've all been there. The good news is, if this happens to you there is a tried-and-true excuse that every pickler can surely relate to. Just say, "I'm normally much better, but today I was just so gosh darn inconsistent."

Did You Know?

A Pickleball court is twenty by forty-four feet, which is the same size as a doubles badminton court.

"MY DINKS WEREN'T DINKING."

It was a tragedy of epic proportions, I tell you! My dinks—those delicate, feather-light shots meant to gracefully arc over the net—had suddenly decided they were on strike. Instead of gently grazing the opponent's side of the court and staying nice and low, they were jumping off the court like high jumpers at the Olympics.

I blame it on the cosmic alignment or a rogue Pickleball fairy with a mischievous streak. Perhaps my dinks were simply feeling misunderstood and wanted to express themselves in a more . . . dramatic fashion.

But fear not, fellow Pickleball enthusiasts, for I have a plan. I shall embark on a quest to woo my dinks back onto my side with promises of glory and admiration. And mark my words, when they return, they shall dink like never before, leaving my opponents in awe! In the meantime, I'll just tell anyone that will listen, "My dinks simply weren't dinking today."

Excuses

"THE BALL HAD A CRACK IN IT."

If you haven't gathered by now, I'm clearly an excellent Pickleball player. But like most maestros, I demand perfection. From the proper preparation, appropriate etiquette, and of course the exact right equipment.

If anything is amiss, it will throw off the balance of my genius just as if a butterfly's inadvertent flap of its wing can change the course of history. So clearly, when that little plastic ball bounces off the well-swept court (it better be clean!), I know exactly where my next shot will go.

But what happens if things go completely haywire and there is an imperceptible crack in the ball . . . heaven forbid?

Well, at least you can explain your missed shot with, "A perfectionist like me clearly can't play up to my incredibly high standards with a crack in the ball."

"THERE WAS A CRACK ON THE COURT."

Similarly to the last excuse, what if there is a crack in the court? Although it's shocking that the world doesn't agree with me that resurfacing Pickleball courts every year is money well spent, some selfish people will argue that they already pay enough in taxes and repaving the public Pickleball courts annually is not their top priority.... I just don't get it.

And if you've been playing long enough, you've likely also noticed that when the courts settle over time, they may eventually produce a crack or two.

While this may seem obscene when the ball lands on this defect and goes awry amid a beautiful game, you can at least use it to your benefit by stating, "How can I be expected to play well when the ball is constantly landing on cracks and going off course?"

"It Just Rained and the Court Was Still Wet."

Ah, it's an infamous excuse, a gem in the treasure trove of Pickleball's best excuses. The sun is peeking through the clouds, the court glistening with the promise of a thrilling match, when suddenly, a few droplets defy the odds and descend from the sky right before you're about to take the stage. In a stroke of comedic timing, I seize the moment, dramatically slipping and sliding across the court like a cartoon character on a banana peel.

Yet, with impeccable timing and a flair for the dramatic, I blame the rain for my ungraceful tumble, eliciting chuckles and eye rolls from their opponents. Was it a genuine slip or a masterful performance worthy of an Oscar? You may never know, but one thing's for sure: when it comes to Pickleball excuses, a solid explanation is, "If I hadn't slipped, I surely would have won the match."

"The Sun Got In My Eyes."

I ask you, fellow Pickleball enthusiast, is there anything better than playing this great game on a beautiful, sun-soaked day? The sky is blue, the birds are chirping, and there isn't a cloud to be seen.

So, I'm playing aggressively, and make my way to the net to stick a hard volley only to have my opponent weakly throw up a lob when I get ready for the kill. And then it happens.

I look straight up into that bright celestial star. With spots in my eyes, I swing wildly and strike nothing but air as the ball comes down and bonks me directly on my noggin.

With my fellow picklers laughing so hard they're gasping for air, I muster all of the integrity I can and say, "You're lucky the sun got in my eyes. Otherwise, you'd have gone down faster than a middle-aged boy band's career."

"My Opponent Got So Lucky."

You see, it wasn't my fault. It was the Pickleball gods playing a prank on me.

My opponent, bless their heart, happened to trip over their own shoelaces. Their paddle flew into the air and the handle perfectly connected with the ball, resulting in a miraculous shot that somehow managed to land within the court lines.

Yes, it was a stroke of luck so profound that even the spectators couldn't help but chuckle. So, you see, it wasn't my lack of skill or strategy. It was just a cosmic convergence of improbable events orchestrated by the mischievous Pickleball spirits. So, if something similar happens to you, just explain with, "Wow, I've never seen such luck!"

Did You Know?

Pickleball uses a solid paddle made of either wood, flax fiber, or toxic oils like carbon fiber.

Excuses

"My Opponent's Mishit Fooled Me."

As I lunged for the perfect shot, my opponent's mishit sent the ball sailing in a wild, unpredictable arc. But here's the kicker: it wasn't the mishit that threw me off. No, it was the sheer audacity of it! I mean, who expects their opponent to be *that* lucky and hit the ball with such unorthodox finesse?

So, there I was, frozen in disbelief, watching as the ball made a beeline for my face like it had a personal vendetta before suddenly changing course and landing squarely right inside the lines. I tried to dodge it, but my body was too busy processing the absurdity of the situation. By the time I snapped out of my daze, I was face-to-face with defeat and a very smug opponent.

Lesson learned: Never underestimate the power of a mishit to completely bamboozle your game plan! But of course, feel free to explain it with, "My opponent's fortuitous mishit left me completely fooled."

"My Opponent Was Dinking Too Much."

As much as I'd love to claim victory with my rush-and-crush mentality, I'm afraid I must confess: my opponent was dinking too much! Yes, you heard it right. Every time I pummeled the ball with my massive power, there it was, the soft tap of the ball just over the net, mocking me with its graceful descent. It was like playing against a Zen-like guru armed with a Pickleball paddle!

I mean, come on! Who can perform at their best with all that dinking going on? It's like trying to play a serious game of Pickleball while your brain is singing nursery rhymes! I couldn't help but be mesmerized by the rhythmic *thud, thud, thud* of the dink.

So, next time you see me on the court, just remember it's not that I lack skill, it's just that my opponent's dinking game is on a whole other level. But of course, if you find yourself in a similar situation, just say, "Oh, that despicable dink!"

"I THOUGHT IT WAS YOURS."

Picture this: The ball comes flying towards me at warp speed, and in a split-second decision, I let it sail right by, convinced it was headed for my partner. I even yell, "Yours!" at the top of my lungs, just to be polite. But the point was lost on both of us, and it lands square in the middle between my compadre and me as we both stare absently at each other.

So, there you have it! Blame it on my overly generous spirit or my keen sense of sportsmanship. Next time, I'll make sure to double-check whose ball it really is before I let it go. I'll tell my partner, "I thought it was yours."

"The Ball Skipped Off the Line."

Amidst a tense match, my opponent unleashes a killer shot. But not to worry . . . I'm there, ready to fight it off, only to have it ricochet off the line. The opponent's eyes widen in a thrilled surprise, awaiting my retort.

With a straight face, I declare, "The ball skipped off the line!" Cue confusion and perhaps a suspicious glance or two. But hey, who can blame a player for blaming it on a renegade ball?

In the realm of Pickleball, where lines blur and shots can be as unpredictable as the weather, anything is possible! So next time you find yourself in this type of pickle, just remember to say, "If that ball didn't skip off of the line, I surely would have won the point."

Excuses

"I'm Too Out of Shape."

In the heat of a Pickleball match, when every point feels like a marathon, sometimes the truth slips out: "I'm too out of shape!" There I am, red-faced and panting, a baby boomer trying to reclaim their glory days on the field of battle.

With each swing of the paddle, I'm reminded of my neglected gym membership and that extra slice of pizza from last night. As my opponent's shots zip past me like cheetahs on caffeine, I can't help but chuckle at my own expense. Sure, blaming my lack of fitness might seem like a cop-out, but hey, it's better than admitting I don't have the skill, right?

Besides, who needs cardio when you've got a killer serve and a knack for making excuses? So, here's to all the out-of-shape warriors out there, sweating it out on the Pickleball court, one excuse at a time! And be sure to tell your victorious opponent, "If I was twenty years younger, I would have dominated."

Excuses

"I JUST HAD SURGERY."

The classic "I just had surgery" excuse, where every twinge of discomfort suddenly becomes a battle scar from the operating table. As I'm hobbling onto the Pickleball court like a wounded warrior, armed with nothing but a paddle and a prescription, my opponents eye me suspiciously, I proudly declare, "Just had surgery, you know. Nothing major, just a minor procedure to remove a stubborn splinter . . . from my pinky toe!"

Cue sympathetic nods and incredulous stares. With each limp and grimace, I turn my handicap into justification. So, here's to all the post-op players out there, turning their setbacks into sidesplitting excuses. And of course, make sure everyone knows, "I just had surgery. Two weeks from now, I'll play much better."

"I Haven't Stretched Properly."

Stay loose! When my game is plummeting and my muscles are tightening up, I simply blame my lack of coordination on my lack of pre-game stretching. As my opponents raise their eyebrows in disbelief, I confidently declare, "It's not me, it's my uncooperative hamstrings! They're as tight as a jar lid after being stuck in the fridge for a month!"

With each awkward swing, I turn my stiffness into a perfect explanation. Who needs flexibility when you've got the comedic timing of a stand-up comic, right? To all the inflexible players out there, stretching the truth and stretching their excuses one strained muscle at a time, I salute you. You can tell everyone who will listen, "I'm a stiff as an old eskimo in the middle of winter."

Did You Know?

Major Pickleball tournaments have a robust economic impact on host cities, often bringing in millions of dollars through lodging, dining, and other visitor expenses.

"I'm a Slow Starter."

As much as I enjoy my weekend or after-work Pickleball game, nothing gets me more psyched than a tournament at the local club. For weeks, I wait in anticipation and dream of hoisting the trophy at the end of a long day of exciting matches.

But occasionally, I'll draw the number one seed in the first round and before I can say, "Pickled," I'm one and done and sent packing.

The good news is there is a perfect excuse for just such a predicament. Just tell your fellow competitors, "I'm just a slow starter. If I could have gotten through the first round, I surely would have taken home the title."

Pickleball's Best Excuses

"I'M OUT OF PRACTICE."

The "I'm out of practice" excuse, where every missed shot is blamed on a lack of recent playing time, is a great one if you're having a subpar match. You can just tell people your erratic performance is due to a prolonged hiatus from the game. As your opponents exchange knowing glances, you can confidently declare, "It's not me, it's my paddle! It's been feeling neglected in the closet, you see, and it's protesting with every swing!"

With each mishit, I turn my rustiness into reason. So, here's to all the rusty players out there, rustling up excuses one missed shot at a time! And don't forget to say, "After a couple of days of playing again, I'll be back to my usual winning spree."

Excuses

"I Didn't Keep My Eye on the Ball."

It can happen to anyone. That momentary lapse in focus. So, I'm squinting at the Pickleball like it's a UFO sighting, as it sails right past me. With a sheepish grin, I confess to my opponents, "It's not my fault! Did you see that thing? It's faster than Usain Bolt."

Who needs laser-like focus when you've got a handful of excuses at the ready? So, if you're juggling excuses and juggling balls on the Pickleball court one missed shot at a time, try simply stating, "I just need to do a better job keeping my eye on the ball."

"I Had a Bad Breakfast."

One morning, I decided to experiment with my breakfast menu and went for the exotic combination of pickles and peanut butter. Let's just say, my taste buds weren't the only thing left in shock. As I waddled onto the Pickleball court, my stomach was protesting louder than an angry crowd after a bad call. Every serve was a reminder of my questionable culinary choices.

Lesson learned: Stick to cereal next time and leave the pickles for the match. Apologies for my pickle-induced performance, but hey, at least I brought some laughter to the court, and I had a great excuse at the ready: "I had the worst breakfast before the match."

Excuses

"My Footwork Was Awful Today."

As every good athlete can attest, footwork is an integral part of the game. If you can get into the proper position before you hit your shots, the game becomes child's play. Yet, if your feet aren't cooperating, that easy groundstroke or volley can become an impediment to your path to the gold.

So, what happens when you're prancing around the court like you have two left feet? Not to worry. After you go down in *de-feet*, just tell your smug opponent, "You may have won today, but if it weren't for my poor footwork, I would have walked all over you."

"I'm Tired from My Morning Run."

If you caught me yawning mid-game like a sleepy bear, here's the scoop: This morning, I thought I'd channel my inner Six Million Dollar Man and hit the pavement for a little jog. Little did I know, my legs were not on the same level as my ambitious brain. What was supposed to be a leisurely jog turned into a ten-mile endurance contest.

By the time I reached the Pickleball court, my legs were protesting louder than a toddler in a candy store. Every swing of the paddle felt like I was battling against a marathon of fatigue. So, if my serves seemed more like gentle lobs and my groundstrokes resembled slow-motion replays, just know it's not lack of fitness or skill—it's the lingering effects of my morning run. And I'll make sure to say, "I shouldn't have run that second five miles before the match today."

"I Have the Worst Case of Pickleball Elbow."

If you're reading this book, it is likely that you are similar to me and simply love the game of Pickleball. And it also wouldn't be a surprise that if, like me, you play any chance you can get. I mean, what is better than spending a full weekend on the courts dinking and ripping?

The downside to all this fun . . . it can lead to some serious injuries, especially if you're on the back nine of life.

"Why not go to the doctor?" you might ask.

Well, that would mean sacrificing time on the court to get poked and prodded by the person in the white coat. So, if you end up hitting the ball and wincing in pain at the same time, just say, "I'm normally much better, but I have the worst case of Pickleball elbow."

Did You Know?

Pickleball combines elements of tennis, badminton, and ping-pong.

"My Hand Was Sweaty and I Couldn't Hold On to the Paddle."

Hear Ye, Hear Ye, fellow Pickleball enthusiasts, allow me to regale you with a tale of woe from the scorching courts of summer at high noon. As the mercury soared, so did my desperation to maintain a hold on my trusty paddle. Alas, my hand resembled a day at the water park, rendering my attempt to play this game at the highest level akin to trying to wrangle a greased pig at a county fair.

With each swing, the paddle threatened to launch itself over the fence. Oh, the indignity of it all! In the sweltering heat, my Pickleball dreams melted away in a split second. So, dear reader, if you seek victory today, blame not your lack of skill but the relentless tyranny of summer's sweaty grasp, and just utter, "I was sweating so profusely I could barely hold on to the paddle."

"SUNSCREEN GOT IN MY EYES AND ON MY HANDS."

Just as I prepared to strike my first shot, a couple of pesky droplets of sunscreen betrayed me, finding their way into my eyes and onto my hands like a mischievous saboteur. Suddenly, my vision blurred, my hands became slippery, and my excuses multiplied faster than the balls flying across the court.

I stumbled, squinting through the irritation, desperately attempting to hold the paddle and regain my focus amidst the relentless rally. Each missed shot became a testament to the treachery of SPF, turning a routine match into an epic battle against a former friend turned foe.

Despite my valiant efforts, victory slipped through my fingers, snatched away by the unexpected assailant—sunscreen, the unlikely nemesis of Pickleball glory. So, next time you see me blinking furiously and wiping my hands on my shirt, just know I'll be shouting, "It wasn't lack of skill, it was the sunscreen."

"I Don't Play Well Against Lefties."

If your opponent is a lefty, well, you've got a great excuse.

With each passing point, it's like they've mastered the art of hitting me where it hurts most: my ego! My backhand becomes an utter mess, my forehand a desperate plea for mercy. I'm spinning in circles, trying to adjust to this mirror-image madness.

As the match progresses, I continue to blame my parents. Why didn't they push me to use my left hand more during my youth?

So, next time you see me losing to a southpaw on the court, just remember, it's not lack of skill, it's the sinister sorcery of left-handedness! But not to worry, you can bet that I'll be explaining my misfortune by stating, "I simply don't play well against left-handed players."

Did You Know?

Pickleball is played internationally, with many countries having their own governing bodies.

Pickleball's Best Excuses

"I'M NORMALLY MUCH BETTER."

One fateful morning, as the game progressed, my skills seemed to evaporate faster than vinegar in the sun. With every missed shot, I found myself blurting out increasingly ludicrous excuses.

I was blaming everything from a sudden aversion to neon plastic balls to a conspiracy involving rogue gusts of wind. My opponents, with eyebrows raised higher than a net post, exchanged skeptical glances. But hey, in the grand game of Pickleball, sometimes you're the cucumber and sometimes you're the brine. And on this particular day, I was swimming in the brine!

So, as I hung up my paddle, I promised myself one thing: Next time, I'll bring my A-game and leave the excuses in the pickle jar where they belong. But until I can redeem myself, I'll surely say, "I just don't know what happened today. I'm normally much better."

"I Need More Lessons."

So, I'm on the Pickleball court, paddle in hand, ready to conquer the world. Or, you know, at least my opponent. However, as the game unfolds, it becomes painfully clear that my paddle might as well be a spatula for flipping pancakes—useless!

With every misguided swing, I find myself muttering, "How am I so bad?!" It's like I'm determined to send every ball into orbit or directly into the net. It's not that I lack talent (at least that's what I keep telling myself), but clearly, I need a little extra guidance from the Pickleball pros.

So, as I shuffle off the court, defeated and discouraged, I make a mental note: next time, more lessons, less flailing. And you can be sure I'll stick by the motto, "A little extra education never hurt anyone."

"I Got a Cramp."

Ah, the dreaded cramp—a pickler's worst nemesis, striking at the most inconvenient moments! There I was, poised for glory, when suddenly, a sharp pain seized my leg, and I collapsed on the court in dramatic fashion.

I could tell my opponents were doubting my cramp, as if I were as good of an actor as a pro soccer player. But hey, who needs skepticism when you've got a perfectly timed excuse, right?

As I massaged my leg, I couldn't help but marvel at the sheer versatility of the cramp excuse. Whether you're losing badly or just need a breather, it's the Swiss Army knife of Pickleball excuses—always reliable, always at your service. Whenever you need it, this excuse is there for you.

So, the next time you find yourself on the brink of defeat, remember the magic words: "I just got the worst cramp!" and then proceed to collapse to the ground.

Excuses

"My Opponent's Outfit Distracted Me."

As I swung my paddle, I couldn't help but notice my opponent's outrageous outfit. Neon colors clashed with polka dots, and a hat the size of a beach umbrella threatened to eclipse the sun. Each time they moved, it was like watching a disco ball ricochet across the court.

I tried to focus, but every time they lunged for a shot, I found myself mesmerized, wondering if they were auditioning for a circus act or a fashion disaster reality show. As the game progressed, I stumbled, missed shots, and even swung and missed completely on several occasions.

When they asked why I was tripping over my own feet, I had to come up with something, so I blurted out, "Your outfit is so mesmerizing, I keep forgetting I'm playing Pickleball and not attending a costume party!"

"My Waistband Broke So My Shorts Kept Falling Down."

If you've been putting on a few extra pounds, perhaps you can relate to this excuse. Imagine this: a Pickleball match where every step I took felt like a high-stakes game of tug-of-war with my shorts. Yep, you guessed it—my waistband decided to throw in the towel, leaving me to fend off gravity's relentless pull. It was like competing in a slapstick comedy, with me desperately trying to maintain dignity while my shorts threatened to make a break for it with every swing.

Forget about footwork; forget about hand eye coordination; forget about skill; I was too busy playing tug-of-war with my own clothing! Opponents may have thought I was doing some bizarre new dance move, but no, it was just my futile attempt to keep my shorts from joining the ranks of the fallen.

Lesson learned: Always double-check the durability of your waistband before hitting the Pickleball court. However, if you do find yourself in this type of precarious position, just say, "They just don't make clothing like they used to."

"I Broke a Shoelace."

So, there I was, dominating as usual, when the unthinkable happened. Out of nowhere, I heard a *snap*. As the tension dissipated from my shoe, I knew I was in trouble. Can you say Tanya Harding 2.0?

Clearly, I was never in the Boy Scouts, so the motto, "Be prepared" was lost on me. Without another pair of shoelaces, I had no recourse but to flounder around on the court with my one good shoe.

Needless to say, the rest of the match didn't go very well, and my opponent stuck a fork in me because I was done. Not to worry, however, because I was sure to tell everyone who was within ear shot, "They clearly don't make shoelaces the way they used to."

Did You Know?

The city of Naples, Florida, is the Pickle capital of the world. Every year, the city hosts the US Pickleball Open Championships.

"My Headband Was Too Tight."

As I lowered my headband over my forehead, it squeezed like a vise grip, constricting tighter with each heartbeat. It was supposed to keep the sweat out of my eyes, but instead, it was cutting off circulation to my brain. I could practically hear my thoughts gasping for air.

With each serve, my vision blurred, my movements slowed, and my opponent's shots seemed to morph into elusive mirages. Was that ball even real, or was it just a figment of my imagination?

When my opponent asked why my color was off, I had to confess, "It's a well-known fact that cranial constriction leads to cognitive confusion and/or poor performance. I was so preoccupied trying to maintain consciousness that I couldn't focus on the game!" And so, I told it like it is: "My headband was way too tight!

"I HAVE ATHLETE'S FOOT."

As I shuffled onto the Pickleball court, I couldn't ignore the itchiness between my toes. The dreaded athlete's foot had struck at the worst possible moment, turning my normally fancy footwork into a comical dance of discomfort. With each step, I felt like I was tiptoeing on hot coals instead of a smooth court.

As the game progressed, my movements became increasingly erratic. Every time I took a step to return a shot, I winced in agony, my mind more focused on the burning sensation than on the game itself.

Turns out, Pickleball and fungal infections don't mix well. Who knew? But at least I could say, "I have the worst case of athlete's foot!"

"I Have a Blister."

In the Pickleball excuse hall of fame, few have achieved such legendary status as the blister. The sun is shining, the opponents are fierce, and there I stand, ready to unleash my Pickleball prowess. But, in the midst of the game, my racket starts to rub against my palm, and a tiny blister appears, as if summoned by the very gods of inconvenience.

It's like a tiny protest from my hand against this intense game. And thus begins the epic saga of how a minuscule blister becomes the antagonist of my Pickleball journey, thwarting serves and groundstrokes, intercepting volleys and overheads, and turning a simple game into a blistering battle of wills. And these are not limited to your hands either! Just wait until your sock bunches up in your shoes!

But now you've got a great excuse. So, just make sure to say, "This little blister was the sole reason for my massive defeat."

"I'm Too Old."

As the Pickleball court becomes my stage, I embrace the excuse that defines my age: With a theatrical sigh and a melodramatic limp, I regale my opponents with tales of yesteryear when I could leap like a gazelle and smash like a titan.

"I may be older than the hills," I declare with a wink, "but don't underestimate the power of experience!" With each stroke, I exude wisdom and cunning, turning my apparent weakness into a strategic advantage.

But alas, my body continues to break down. Father Time is undefeated. And sure, I'm no match to an opponent half my age. As I shake hands with the young whippersnapper, I'm sure to tell her, "Youth surely is wasted on the young."

Excuses

"I Made Too Many Mental Errors."

The Pickleball court is a battleground of wit and skill. I find myself ensnared in the treacherous trap of mental errors. With each misplaced shot and mistimed move, I cry out in dismay, "Ah, the dreaded brain fog strikes again!"

As I recount tales of my mind's misadventures, from forgetting the score to confusing my left from my right in the heat of battle, my opponents appear dubious.

But fear not, fellow Pickleball aficionados, for amidst the chaos of my mental gymnastics, there lies a nugget of wisdom: "It's not the size of the error, but the hilarity of its aftermath that truly defines a Pickleball match!" And with this sentiment in mind, when you're drowning your woes with a cold one after the match, be sure to say, "I just don't know where my mind was today."

"My Opponent Claimed the Point Just Because I Threw My Paddle at Her."

Can you believe that my enemy across the net claimed the point just because I threw my paddle at her? But hear me out—I swear it was an involuntary reflex! You see, I was so immersed in the intense rhythm of the game that my paddle decided it wanted to explore the spot right between my opponent's eyes. Aiming for the perfect lob shot, the paddle misjudged its trajectory and flew from my hand, landing right in the middle of my opponent's path.

Naturally, I stood, bewildered, trying to explain to my irate opponent that it wasn't purposeful. It was my powerful swing and competitive fierceness that resulted in a shot to her chops. Lesson learned: Next time, I'll make sure to reel in my exuberance before the game! And if this ever happens to you, feel free to tell your competitor, "Oops, my paddle slipped from my grasp!"

"MY OPPONENT WAS IN THE ZONE."

At a recent match I was met with a sight so astonishing, it blew my socks off: My opponent, usually a mix of clumsiness and confusion, had transformed into a Pickleball prodigy overnight.

With each serve, it was as if they had been possessed by the spirit of a Pickleball god, gracefully placing shots with pinpoint accuracy. My attempts at returning the ball resembled a futile attempt at anything closely resembling athleticism.

In the end, defeated and bewildered, I had no choice but to offer up the classic excuse: "I've never seen my opponent play that well!" After all, how else could I explain the sudden transformation from bumbling beginner to Pickleball virtuoso? But not to worry, because you can bet after the match I was shouting from the rooftops, "There was nothing I could do. My opponent was in the zone."

Did You Know?

Joel Pritchard, Bill Bell, and Barney McCallum invented the sport because they couldn't find any shuttlecocks to play badminton.

"MY PARTNER IS A COURT HOG."

Ever been in a Pickleball match where your partner seems to have rented out the entire court for a solo performance? That was my predicament on many occasions.

From the first serve, my partner dashed around the court like a caffeinated Tasmanian Devil, leaving me with nothing but the scraps of shots that squeaked past their monopolizing paddle. They lunged, leaped, and pirouetted across the court, convinced they were auditioning for the Pickleball version of *Swan Lake*.

No matter how much I pleaded for a chance to hit the ball, they were focused solely on their own glory. I complained to anyone who would listen, hoping they'd understand the struggle of being overshadowed by a Pickleball prima donna.

In the end, I blamed it on their insatiable appetite for court dominance and made sure to tell everyone within earshot, "We would have won if my partner wasn't such a court hog!"

"We Both Called 'I Got It.'"

Picture this: a crucial moment in a heated Pickleball match. The ball is sailing gracefully through the air, and in a split second, both my partner and I shout in unison, "I got it!"

What follows is a scene straight out of a slapstick comedy. We collide mid-air, limbs flailing, and crash to the ground in a tangle of paddles and wristbands.

As we lay there, dazed and tangled, it became clear that our synchronized enthusiasm had backfired spectacularly. "We both called for it," I mumble to the bewildered spectators, hoping they'll understand the absurdity of our predicament.

In the end, we blame it on our overly enthusiastic team spirit and vow to work on our communication skills before our next match. But hey, at least we provided some unintentional entertainment and had a built-in excuse, "We both called, 'I got it!'"

"I Should Have Stuck to Tennis."

Like many Pickleball enthusiasts, I got my start on the tennis court. After years of running from the baseline to the net, and from one alley to the other, I thought there must be an easier way. The smaller Pickleball court seemed like a terrific alternative.

Unfortunately, my powerful groundstrokes and overhand serve didn't translate as well as I had hoped. And after rushing and crushing into the kitchen for my umpteenth penalty, and getting dinked to death, I realized that there is a lot more to this game than "mini-tennis."

So, I gave it my best shot. I watched videos, took lessons, and practiced, practiced, and practiced some more. But inevitably, I realized this seemingly simple game was much more complex than I thought. So, at the end of the day, as I walked away with my tail between my legs, I simply said, "I never should have thrown out my tennis racket."

Epilogue

So always remember, my fellow Pickleball enthusiast, do your best. Try your hardest. Fight to the bitter end. And as long as you come to the court equipped with your sneakers, paddle, sunscreen, water bottle, and this little book packed snuggly in your bag, you're sure to be prepared. Yet, if the unthinkable occurs, and you lose the most important point of the match, the final point, you'll have nothing to fear. Just open this book to the page with the appropriate excuse and explain away your woeful play with a gem from *Pickleball's Best Excuses.*

Acknowledgments

To my mother and biggest cheerleader, Sylvia Shifrin, who told me for years that *Pickleball's Best Excuses* was a great idea for a book. I'm happy I finally listened. Thanks, Mom!

About the Author

Joshua Shifrin earned his bachelor's degree from Clark University in Worcester, Massachusetts where he majored in psychology. He then earned his master's degree in Educational Psychology and his specialist degree in School Psychology. After working as a school psychologist for approximately five years, Joshua went on to obtain his PhD in Counseling and School Psychology from Florida State University.

Joshua is now a licensed psychologist and author. He currently maintains a private neuropsychology practice where he specializes in working with school-aged students.

Joshua has always had a love for the written word, and he writes wherever, and whenever, he can find the time. Joshua lives in New Jersey with his wife and two boys. *Pickleball's Best Excuses* is the fifth book in his Sports Excuse series and his twentieth book overall.

Also Available by Joshua Shifrin

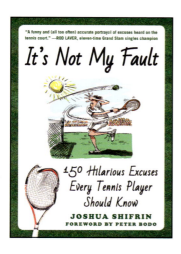

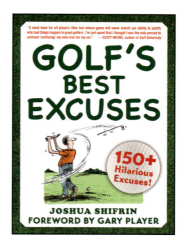

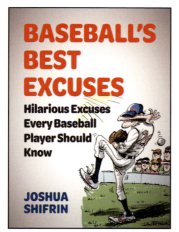

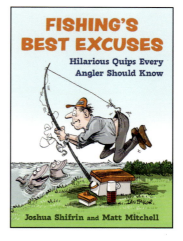